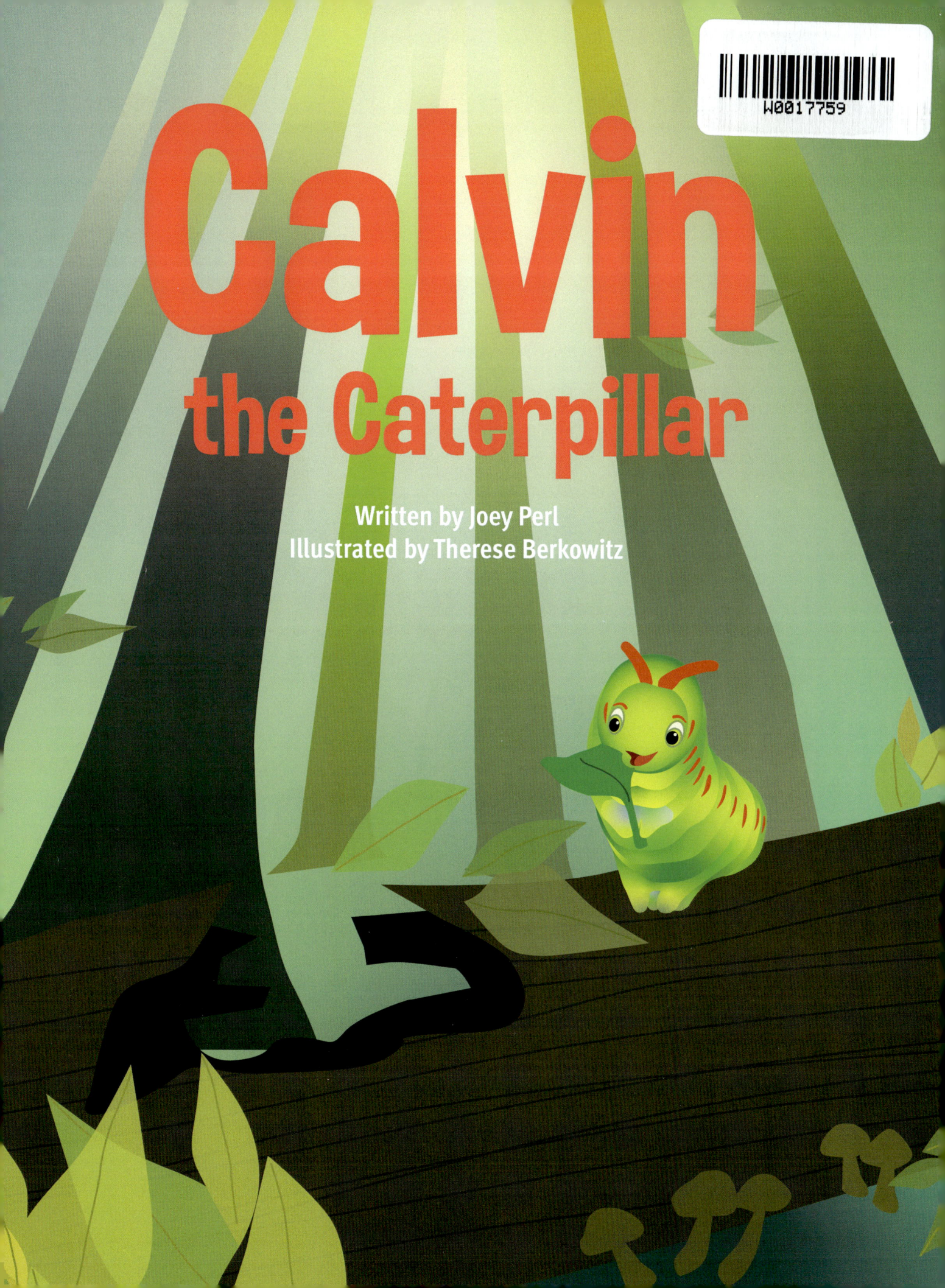

Calvin
the Caterpillar

Written by Joey Perl
Illustrated by Therese Berkowitz

For Levi and Ari.
May you find a life-long friend in each other.
Pursue your goals with passion!

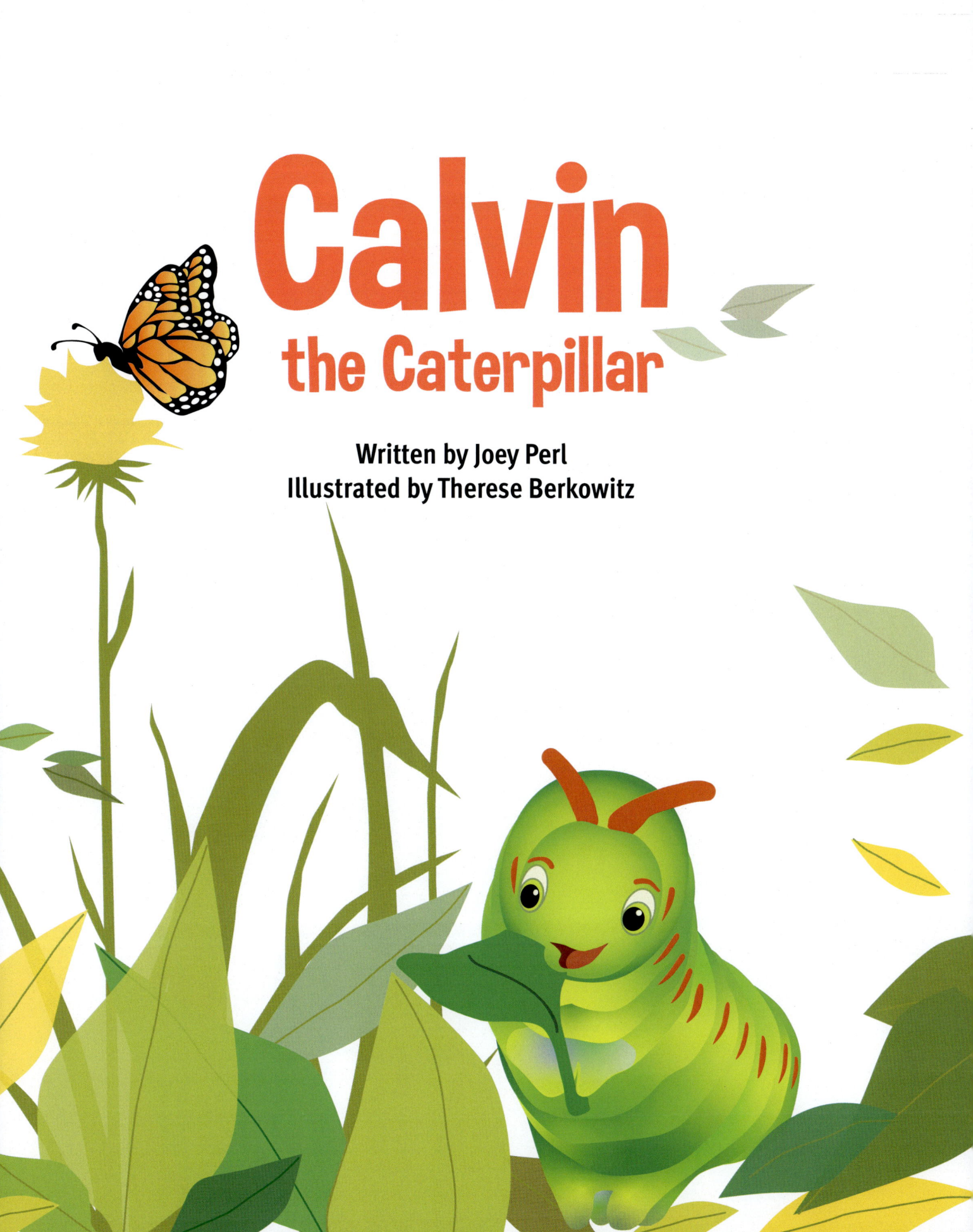

Calvin
the Caterpillar

Written by Joey Perl
Illustrated by Therese Berkowitz

Calvin the Caterpillar was very content.
He wore a big smile wherever he went.

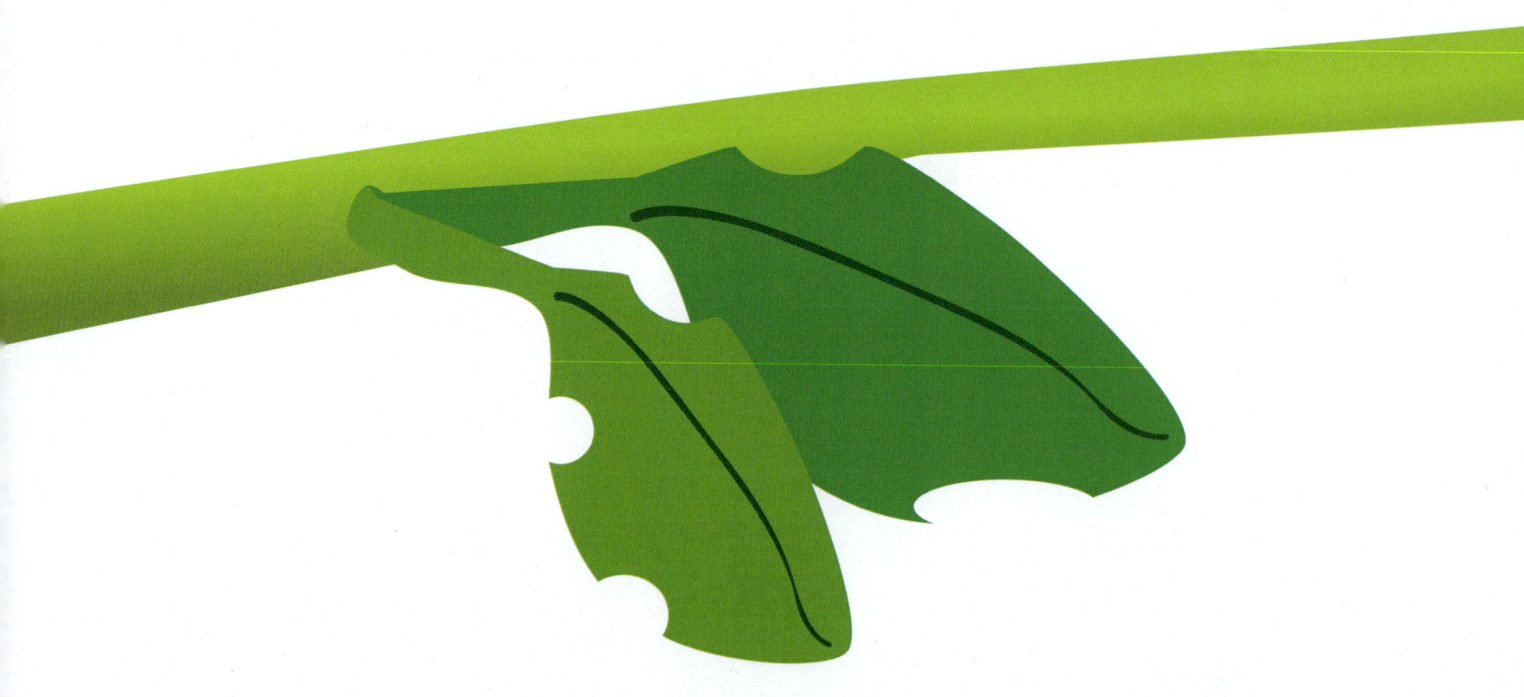

Living on the forest floor, he loved eating leaves.
There were plenty to share for him and Steve.

Steve and Calvin were best of friends.
They would talk about the future for days on end.

Every night they would speak near a tree,
But, no matter how long they spoke,
they would always disagree.

"Caterpillars become butterflies
and it isn't their choice.
I CAN'T WAIT TO FLY," said Steve
in a confident voice.

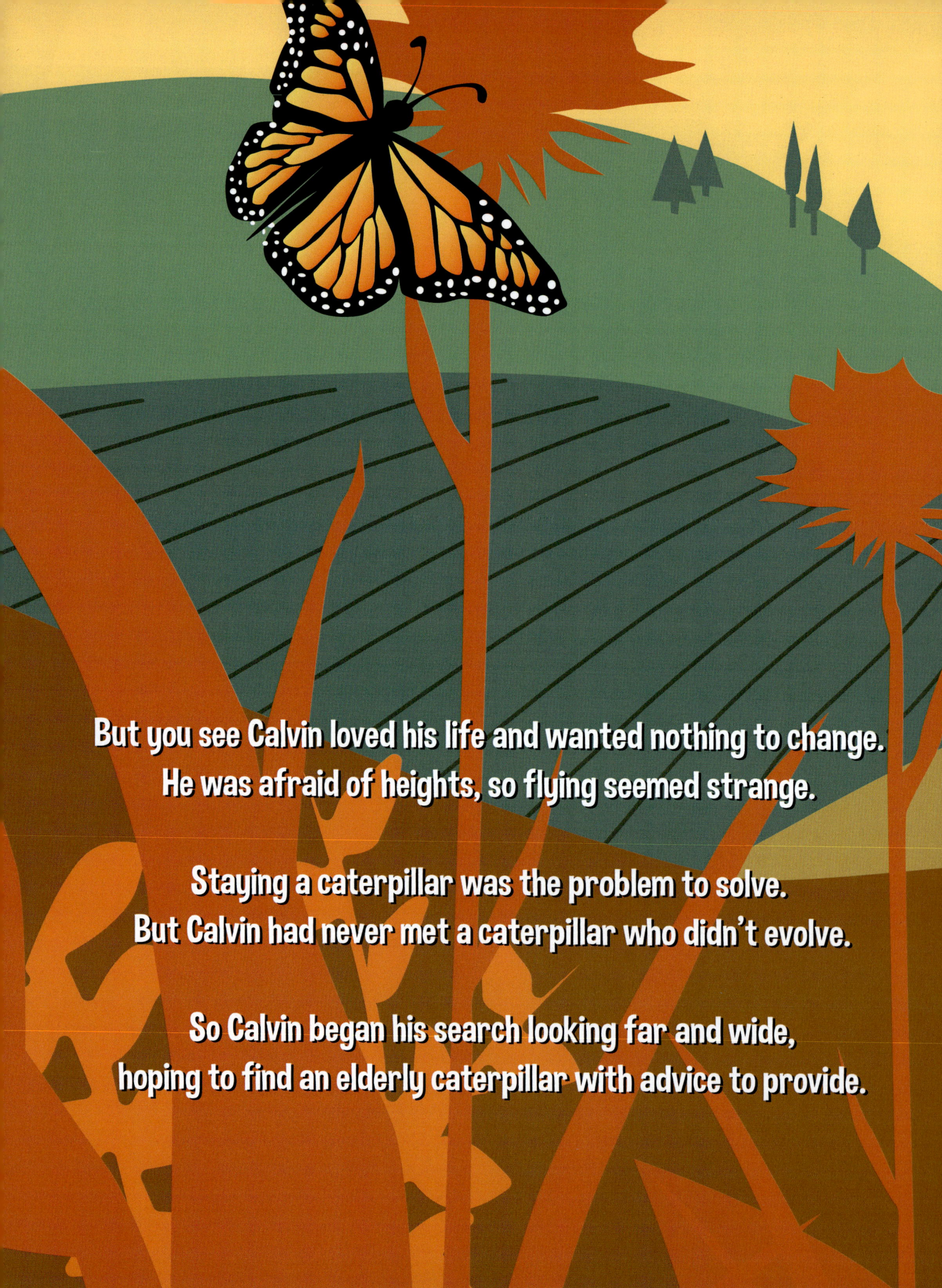

But you see Calvin loved his life and wanted nothing to change.
He was afraid of heights, so flying seemed strange.

Staying a caterpillar was the problem to solve.
But Calvin had never met a caterpillar who didn't evolve.

So Calvin began his search looking far and wide,
hoping to find an elderly caterpillar with advice to provide.

The longer he searched the less answers he had;
He missed his friend Steve, and he was lonely and sad.

The forest was much bigger than Calvin had thought;
He missed being home and the comfort it brought.

Feeling cold and weak
Calvin began to shiver.

At that very moment
he heard a voice near the river.

"Calvin! Calvin! I've missed you, my friend!
We have been friends since the beginning
and will be friends til the end."

"Steve, I'm so happy you're here!!
I couldn't believe my eyes when I saw you appear."

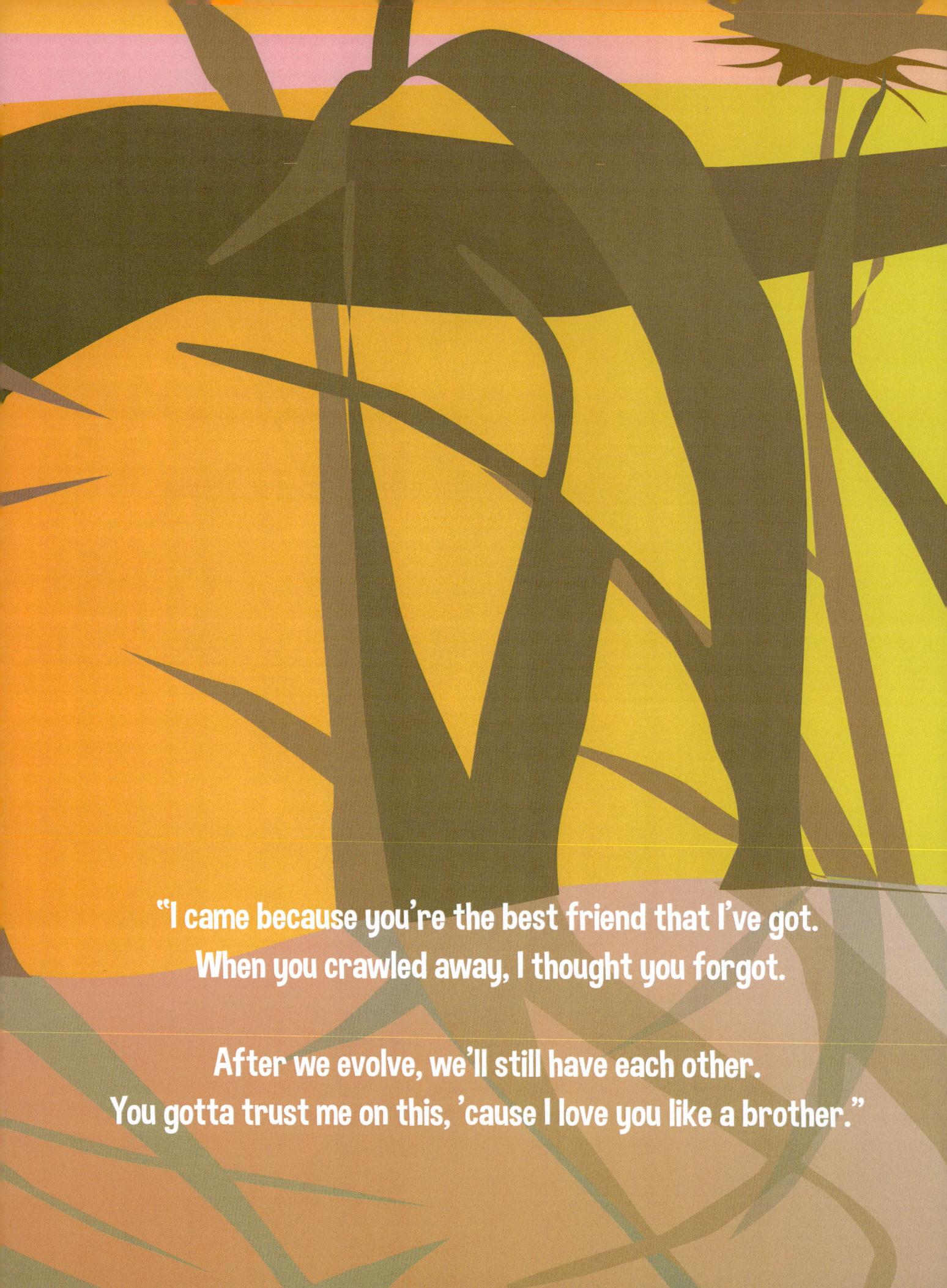

"I came because you're the best friend that I've got.
When you crawled away, I thought you forgot.

After we evolve, we'll still have each other.
You gotta trust me on this, 'cause I love you like a brother."

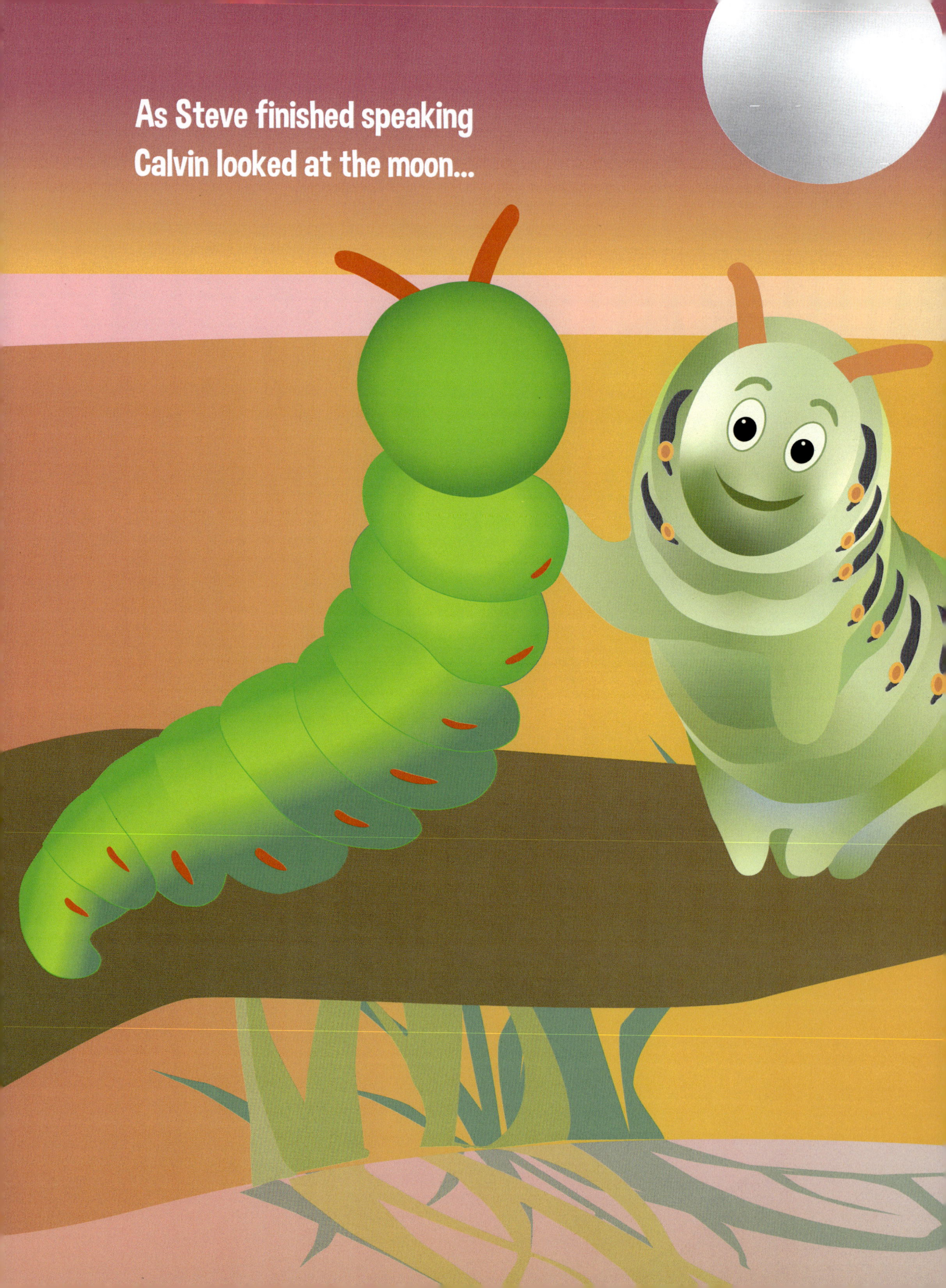

As Steve finished speaking
Calvin looked at the moon...

"...The next thing that he knew,
he was in a cocoon!

On that day Calvin learned
a valuable lesson.
Having a best friend like Steve
is a wonderful blessing.

Whether you are human or insect,
things change from time to time,
but if we journey together, we will all be just fine.